THE SEASHORE

Created by Gallimard Jeunesse
and Elisabeth Cohat
Illustrated by Pierre de Hugo

A FIRST DISCOVERY BOOK

Cartwheel
·B·O·O·K·S·®

SCHOLASTIC INC.
New York   Toronto   London   Auckland   Sydney

The area where the sea meets land is called the seashore. The seashore is always changing. At high tide, we can't see much of the shore. At low tide, the sea rolls back and we see more of the shore.

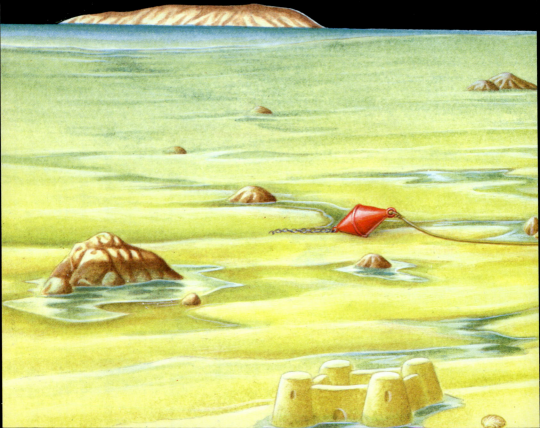

There are rocky shores, muddy shores,
and sandy shores.
All kinds of animals live on the shore.
When the tide goes out, you can see some
animals living in the open.
Others are hidden.

As soon as the tide goes out,
crabs scurry under rocks
and shellfish bury themselves
in the sand.

Be kind to the animals
that live here. Replace
any rocks that you lift.
Don't turn them around
or upside down.

No matter what its shape or size,
a crab has ten legs.
Can you count them?

It moves
sideways with
eight of its legs.
The other two legs,
called pinchers,
are folded
in front.

The crab is called a crustacean
because it has a horny covering or "crust."

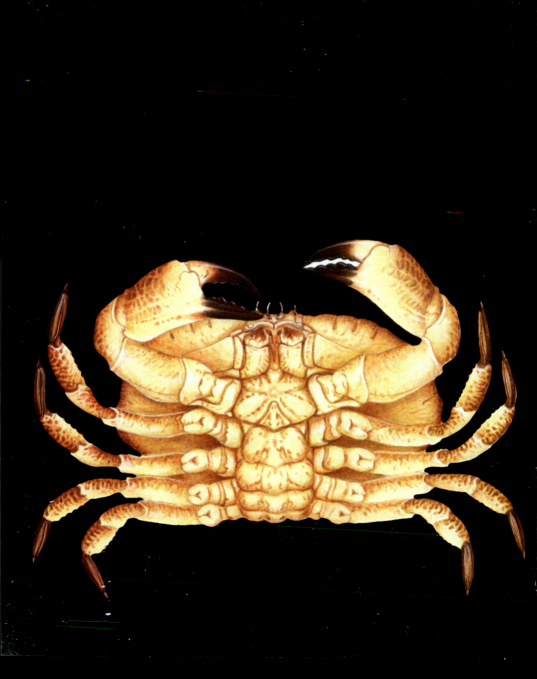

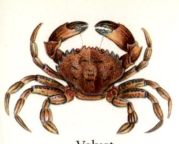

Velvet
swimming crab

Sand crab

Common
shore crab

With its
pinchers, it seizes
food like this sea
urchin, tears it into
pieces, and brings it
to its mouth.

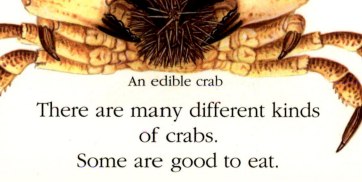

An edible crab

There are many different kinds
of crabs.
Some are good to eat.

The lobster has
a long body.
Watch out for its
powerful claws!

The spiny
spider crab
has long, skinny
legs.

Crabs, shrimp, and
lobsters are all crustaceans.

Shrimp

Sand hopper

Squat
lobster

Hermit crabs have soft
bodies. They live inside
empty shells.

When they grow
bigger, they move
into a bigger shell.

Who is hiding
inside this shell?

The sea anemone looks like a plant but it is an animal. Underwater, it attaches itself firmly to a rock. Its tentacles snatch nearby shrimp for food.

When the tide goes out, the anemone
pulls in its tentacles.
It can live out of the water this
way until the next high tide.

An oyster attaches itself
to a rock by its "foot."

Mussels attach themselves
by their "beards."

Oysters, mussels,
and scallops are called
mollusks. Their soft bodies
are protected by hard shells.

Some mollusks, like scallops,
are divided into two parts or "valves"
that open and close. The scallop moves by
clapping its valves together.

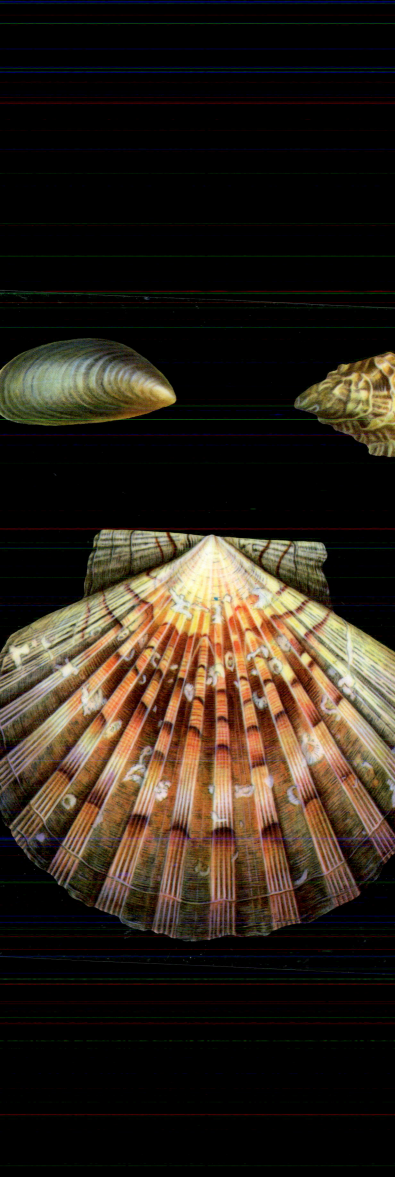

Mussel

Oyster

Let's look inside.

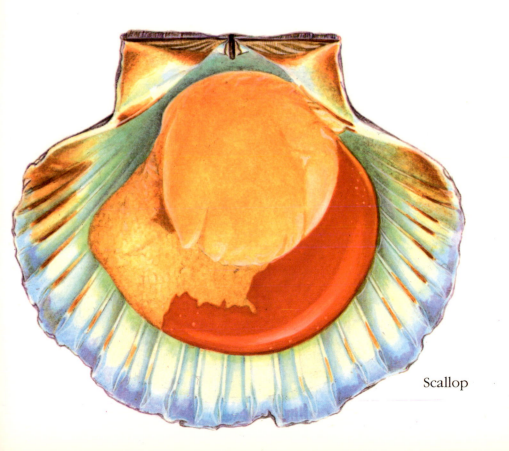

Scallop

Starfish and sea
urchins have no
heads, but they
have mouths on
their bellies.

A starfish uses
its long arms
to walk around.

What does the sea
urchin look like
under its spines?

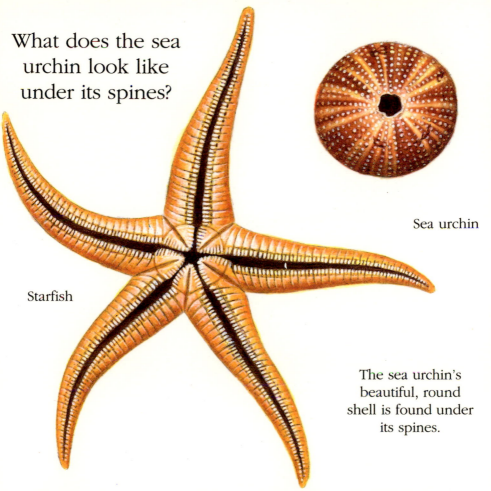

Sea urchin

Starfish

The sea urchin's
beautiful, round
shell is found under
its spines.

The common starfish has five flexible, fragile
arms with rows of tiny tube feet underneath.
The tip of each foot has a suction disk that
helps the animal to crawl and to catch food.

Sand eels

At low tide,
you can fish for sand eels
by digging in the wet sand
with a rake.

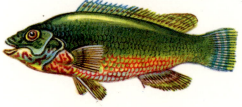

Wrasse

Other fish stay safe at low tide
by hiding in the seaweed.

Common
goby

Who is hiding in
the seaweed?

Moray eel

The moray eel
hides between the rocks
and pops its head out,
hoping to catch prey to eat.

At birth, these fish have an eye
on each side of their head.
As they grow, they become flat and
both eyes move to the same side.

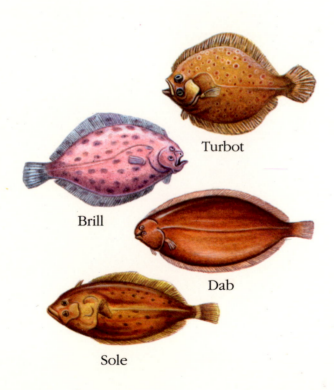

Turbot

Brill

Dab

Sole

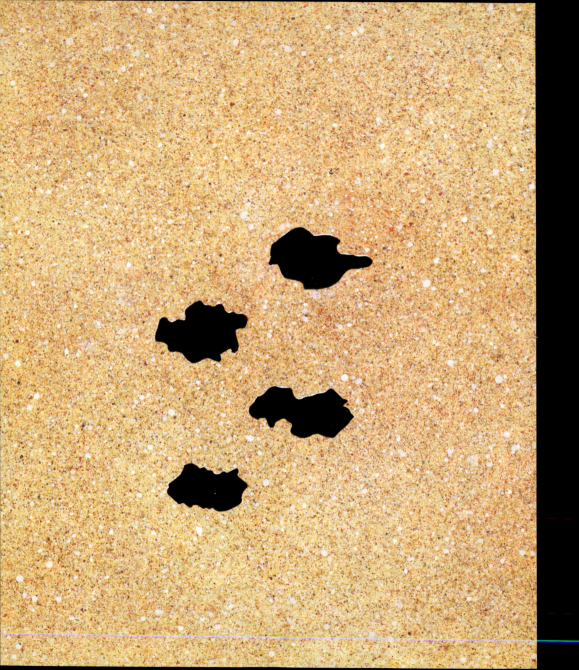

When the plaice
hides in the sand,
it is almost impossible
to find.

Plaice

Parents Magazine
"Best Books" Award

**Parenting Magazine*
Reading Magic Award

***Oppenheim Toy Portfolio*
Gold Seal Award

Library of Congress Cataloging-in-Publication Data available.

Originally published in France under the title *Le Bord de la Mer* by Editions Gallimard.

ISBN 0-590-20303-7

12 11 10 9 8 7 6 5 4 3   5 6 7 8 9/9 0/0
Printed in Italy by Editoriale Libraria
First Scholastic printing, March 1995